UNRHYMEFIED

FRACTIONAL MUSINGS

JYOTISHRAJ THOUDAM

To

Dad,

Those who stayed,

Those whose heart did not sway when that part of me sailed with the wrong wind,

Those who knows the true meaning of loving someone unconditionally,

Those who left from my life too

Those who made me stronger

Contents

Foreword — vii

Preface — ix

Acknowledgements — xi

Prologue — xiii

1. Unrhymefied — 1

2. Flower — 3

3. Process — 4

4. Progress — 5

5. Perfections — 6

6. Imperfections — 7

7. Mood Games — 8

8. Hang On — 9

9. Until Then — 10

10. Poets — 11

11. Right — 12

12. Naturals — 13

13. Fear? — 14

14. Choice — 16

15. Zoo-pology — 18

16. Her — 19

17. Love — 20

18. Life Part-1 — 21

19. Life — 22

20. Lying — 24

21. Break — 25

22. Morning Laziness — 26

Contents

23. Evidence & Faith 27

Epilogue 29

Foreword

I am still not worthy of writing a forward, until then, I leave this page with three blahs.

three blahs.

blah, blah & blah.

Preface

Before the actual preface, here's an important history to be noted as it serves the right path to completely acknowledge the work of poetries here, from past and the present. So!

It was a rainy night in January when all things came into light. January 9, 2022 is a special day for me. The things that occured and connections which I was able to make is even for me quite surreal. I did not experience much emotions of satisfaction but the hunger continue to grow to see what more could be done to complete the quest for new language too. Long after in April, I gave it a title called "A theory of learning ..." etc.

Now the above is said and done, the body of work compiled here is meant to be an appreciation and for some, an apology. As my recognition of the truth based on reliable facts which I have gathered from various sources.

The name of the book does not exist as a word in the dictionary, here I intend to give meaning as "a collection of poems which the poet is unaware of the patterns of poetry." Isn't that what we humans do? Invent something that do not exist and give meanings or values to things. That is the intended effect.

Also the peacock is India's national bird, which I wanted her to carry my book by her magestic "wings of fire" :) to all those writers who are afraid to write, who are afraid of shame and the hypochondriactic disease called "writer's block"

A rose in the winter background is no surprise which I intend to show that the fragility of a man's or a woman's heart can withstand even the coldest of response or act. That there is still hope, that the peacock is at your back, dear roselyn :)

Jyotishraj Thoudam

6:45 AM 23 July 2022

Imphal West, Manipur

Acknowledgements

Even though I wrote almost all the poems in my free time, the time that was freed due to a lot of help by the following people.

Starting from the not so obvious, I would like to thank coffee. For that beaverage of a girl helps me gather the thoughts. From the most dumbest version to the witty ones, that I was able to string words and form melancholic sentences.

Mom & Dad, they're my never ending joy and will appear almost in every page of any acknowledgment.

Furthermore, I would be foolish not to mention my close cousins/bloods, Banabanta Ngangom, Sangeeta Ngangom, Purnima Ngangom, Sonia Ngangom, Zenith Guruaribam, Iteima/Bhabhi Charu Paliwal, Bablu Leirenlakpam, Brilenia Lairenlakpam, Sandeep Lairenlakpam, Iteima Anil Bala Lairenlakpam & my aunts from Wangbal Mayai Leikai, namely, Aunt Thoudam Santama, Aunt Thoudam (O) Ibecha, Aunt Thoudam (O) Thoinu, Nidhi Shamurailatpam, Saroj Kumar Guruaribam, Landhoni Guruaribam, Brajakumar Ngangom, Hemani Ngangom, Giri Bala Ngangom, for without their support at my time of ail would have been another path.

My close friends Ranjan Leishangthem, Gurumayum Madan Mohan Sharma, Ningthemcha Mayum Ranjan, Ranju Mayanglambam, Dhanakumar Elangbam, Kumarjit Khundrakpam, Nikheel Mangang, Dr. Keveena Thingujam, Prasanna Padma Raj Kulkarni, Shreya Singh Rajpoot, Sugandha Singh, & the Alfaz group of IITGN for I have gained more life lessons & the support by interacting with them until the writing of this acknowledgement.

A team of doctors which I became friends when they helped me see the light through a tough period of my time, Dr. Awrushim Muivah, Dr. Samson

ACKNOWLEDGEMENTS

Sangma, Dr. Ahel Banerjee, Dr. Daniella Longjam, Dr. Pertin Talom, Dr. Chanu Konsam, Dr. Julia Wahengbam, for them I dedicated the 7th poem in this work.

And the whole team of IITGN community of Professors, explicitly mentioning some, my guide Professor Dilip Sundaram, Professor Kabeer Jesuja, Professor Arnapurna Rath, Professor Prasanna Venkatesh, Security head Biresh Chaubey for this period of my writing.

Prologue

Writing is difficult. But when we start typing a word, a sentence and then soon comes the full stop. Writing is like speaking, you want to talk more as soon as you start talking, you never get enough of writing.

So jump in and start writing.

Be it rhymed or unrhymed poems, let your heart write it first and then your mind will follow.

Most of the poems are a direct line from the heart, unfiltered and some from the mind, that too filled with witty remarks.

I hope you enjoy it, and seeing some of my, I'm not gonna lie, shitty writing, you can begin your own journey! Have fun!

1. Unrhymefied

Poetry is a wonderful journey for the human heart,

And it is a pleasure to be seen, from the deepest depths and the many

chaos,

The untied letters and words, these unrhymed verses,

Do I write.

I cannot say nor speak the many thoughts at times,

But yes do I find the peace in poetifying or knowing it out,

Perhaps this play of the words is a kind of the truth,

But many have said that there is more to be seen than what meets the eye.

Yes it is dark and I am not asleep,

Awake and stringing these words from the dark,

Maybe it has no meaning till now, 'fore 'tis writ it flew in air,

But the moment I inked, it became unclear yet the smudged is still a

worthy sight.

Maybe the test is to do and not to think,

Maybe to think is not only to write or to write need less of a worthy

mind,

But only the heart and memory are crucibles of meaning's end or

beginning,

Perhaps we fear too much of shame and shunned,

But without a mind free of fear will not succeed,

In living a life with adventure filled, or perhaps the assigning meanings to

events,

Yet the voices of a poet never did call for war,

Only a call for peace and lament of deeds and thoughts.
I can be wrong and this meets no true regard,
But a thing can only be certain with a beginning of the thought,
A thought free of shackles to write,
And write even the unrhymed verse, without an inkling's care from the
voice of the world.

(4:10 AM 23/07/2022)

2. Flower

Someone gave me a test,
Hope I survive this entourage of a view,
Perhaps the bees understand more than I do,
The meaning behind the scent.
Can't reveal her name or the rest,
Cause we all know roses in lieu,
Got thorns, prickly than most bees do,
Not aiming for perfection, these words I've rent.
But yes, flowers aint what I aim to collect.
But those, shower of colors do I am to lament.

(10:37 PM, 11 July 2022)

3. Process

Things, relationships, work and hope, a process,
No one has escaped its wall,
The first, through the wall, bloody as always.
Having lived through many a wall,
Immaculately, enumerate, elaborate, I can, those ways.
Perhaps, this process, avoided, we will, fall,
Undoing what is must, shoulds and wants, it goes away,
For the future waits for no man with much gall.
For the future belongs, to those who fight on the D-Day.
Messy, it always is in the middle of it.
Heck! the passionate will tell you, in the end it is lit.
Lazy, it always feels in the beginning.
Heck! Man through wall will tell you, the end will greet you shinning!

(7:55 PM, July 5,2022)

4. Progress

Be it Math, Science or Religion,
We seek progress,
But progress as we've seen, requires a battalion,
Of dedicated connections free from distress.
What philosophers seek is no soft dandelion,
What progress seek is your first cry at stress,
However hard it may seem, it is no caged lion.
Tested with time, it requires will no less,
Coursing through time, it requires diving into oblivion.
Though hard at first, remember higher the wall, sweeter the bless.
Swiftly the delay kicks in, but hey its no stallion,
We must, with equal hearts, with no rest,
Seek help, not for completeness but progress.
Seek peace not pleasure, not for perfection but progress.

(10:23 PM July 5, 2022)

5. Perfections

Funny did I imagine process, progress & perfection,
Well, endings, no more perfect than the beginning,
Said people with trapped imaginings,
Torn between past & the present doings,
Help did I ask, for forgiveness to return as in the beginning.
To grant or not grant, not in my own connections,
Meaning strings or hubris of the defeated,
These words might seem,
I gather, without pain or pleasure, words of wisdom,
To comfort, in the imaginings of the perfected,
Perhaps to my own placidity & peace these perfections.
Those forgotten days, no help in reminiscing,
For closure is not sought for, but what is right,
Word of a friend, kept this alive, these randomly flowing,
These Marathons of perfecting sentences, icing it white.

(10:43 PM, July 5/2022)

6. Imperfections

I like imperfections & mistakes
They make me feel safe
For if it were perfect
And it fails
I would not know how I'd survive
Without knowing the reasons for its failure
For the reasons of the unknown
Is what makes men mad
I would become mad
If not for the imperfections caressed me deeply
As I lay here, in her bosom of carelessness
I could see the light
Through the cracks of these imperfections
Through the thorns of these bleeding mistakes

Shillong, December 15, 2021)

7. Mood games

Been there, done that,
Ups and downs of the mind,
The drama of this chemical brain,
Will play all the games, served up until I snap,
Curved balls and the dunks of the mind,
In the playground, out in the open in pain.
This is a Hi 5! to my saviours,
A thank you to those, who told me,
The rules of this game,
A bow, to those who coached my behaviours,
Wishing you all, a blessed day from thee,
For the things, I overcame.
But this is neither the end nor a closure form.
But this is a claim, a shout-out for making me reborn.

(10:03 PM July, 7,2022)

8. Hang on

Hang on while I ride this one out,
I did tell you stop reading,
But hey, you're here, so help me out,
Save me the trouble of these words popping.
Can't help yourself, can you?
Thinking why I had done this or done that,
Stop and let it settle, remember it's all for you!
Scavenging the remains, my mind wandering out flat,
Among the death poets and the nerdy romans,
Through the Hemingways and Sylvia Plaths,
Inside the Greeks and the Latin humans,
I can't, without feelings, see those paths!
If you're looking for an escape,
I'm here to help you,
To be one's own friend, and let it tap,
Among those mighty thoughts inside you!
Always! Let there be a place of hanging on,
Inevitably, a place of letting go, shall it be born.

(6:07 PM July 5/2022)

9. Until then

Until then I might not see you,
Until then I might not love you,
Have been avoiding love poems for a while,
But I guess thats what real poets do.
But I guess that what the great romantics do.
Until its done, we are never sure,
Until its done, we can never endure,
Have been avoiding this feelings for a while,
But I guess the rhymes don't flow on its own,
But I guess daydreams don't take a life of its own,
Until it's done.
Until then, I am, I was, I will keep this lid on.
Until then, we were, we are, we will ride this one out.

(5:29 PM July 5/2022)

10. Poets

A feeling of letting go and holding on,
Is where the brook of poems lie.
I am not alone,
That fetch from this pond like one of mine.
But cheers to the fact that you are also not alone,
Maybe a song might help it die.
Yet feelings never do crash on their own,
My lost friends, my dear comrades, I cannot lie.
For the memories, good and bad, we did not face it alone.
Expressions never lie, neither do numbers cry.
Expressions never die, neither do words die alone.
Expressions never made poets, neither do thoughts alone.
Without those feelings and outcry,
A poet is never again a whole.

(1:59 PM 5 July 2022)

11. Right

I realized what most people find ugly,
I consider beautiful,
Perhaps this is my bug or maybe a feature,
But I cannot be sure of these surely.
Maybe people miss things the way they are,
But find it hard, to coalesce and just be,
Becuase harder the things, smoother it becomes to ignore,
To fight for what is right, costly, so ignored fully bare.
Forward is the only way, rising from our collective view,
Yet imagines everything in an instant,
Imagination becomes powerful to calm & accept,
Those things which are not, we try it to be yet away they flew.
Perhaps House was right,
Persistence doesn't make you worthy,
Realizing this is hard,
I have accepted it, for it is right.

(11 June 2022)

12. Naturals

I read once
Somewhere in the old books
That what comes naturally
Must not be celebrated
Because what is true achievement
Are those qualities that is earned
Are those principles that is cultivated
Rather than the easy
In that sense
God's work, or naturals
However perfect it maybe, is natural to him
Therefore it must not be celebrated

(IIT Gandinagar - 8:21 AM 5 jan 2022)

13. Fear?

Why do you fear?

Do you fear because of the risk?

Or is it the consequences?

What if I tell you, make friends with the consequences

For she will guide you out of it

For it is a necessary process to face the unknown

And you must be willing to get hurt

It must be felt until you see the new

Even if it takes 3000 hurts

I am willing to risk it

Made a pact with the devil

That even you don't dare to stop me

If I fall, I would fall on the dirt

For it is the dirt that makes the earth

If I die trying, I would have succeeded

Because the devil was scared

For it is the truth, that I tried to grasp

For it is the wisdom, that will rise even in death

You must be willing to take the hits

You must be willing to fail

I did

But it was beautiful, and believe me

It was worth the risk

JYOTISHRAJ THOUDAM

(22 December 2021)

14. Choice

Maybe it is in our choice that defines us,
The choice of words, things, people, plants & habits.
I do not know the vast ocean of philosophy books,
But I do know that I do not know, those serious bits.
Perhaps it is our job to contribute,
As the drops makes plenty of oceans.
To the ocean of knowledge, and strive for a minimum rebuke,
And to the thoughts that could light lanterns.

However perfect it maybe, to the human mind,
We cannot think out of reality.
Certainly castles in the sky is the choice of the blind,
We cannot build bridges of reason, if we believe in destiny.

Perhaps it is too much ask for,
To give up the notion of conventional belief.
Perhaps it our choice to shell ourselves from hurt,
To cover and embalm certain scars of our human leafs.
But one thought alone cannot bring about the power of choice in the mass,
Rather put all hope in the collective forces of the brutes, to gather the delights of choice in every tasks.

(10:43 PM May 2, 2022, Monday)

15. Zoo-pology

Dear animals, abandoned from your native places,
I, without any authority, on behalf of all concerned humans apologize.
I do not know, these bouts of emotional instances,
Are right or wrong, my dears from another species.
But we are all sinners, aren't we?
In the religious sense or not.
Those ramblings of the barb or howlings towards thee,
Perhaps it is pointless to cry or wail among the hilly lofts.
Was it pleasure or pain, when you growled,
I do not know, and perhaps we can never know.
But yes, deep inside, among our being's thoughts ignored,
Freedom must the gift, that we want to adorn you.
I could not help but lament, in I & We,
Being human myself, my voice is in words.
I know it will be just words & lost in being free,
Toss and turn we will debate and discuss, until we realize, it was lost
within the forest of words.
Therefore, I end my valleys and hills of apology letter,
Not knowing how and why change happens for the best or worst and lost,
hoping its not a losing battle for the better.

(May 3ʳᵈ, 2022)

16. Her

Memories of her, hovering inside my mind, so deep,

All jittery and nice, with her touch, so sweet.

Never knew how I missed, quicker than falling asleep,

Was it all hormones, or the numbing sense of heat?

For I could see her, through that wall of anger and insult,

Those pieces of abandoned soul, over millennia of hurt.

Abused and misused, orchestrating a brave conduct,

Strengthened by the bond of her past, she flies inert.

Beneath that face of bravado and swagger,

Was covered with flames, but breathes air to all.

For she knew what it feels like, heart filled with daggers,

Waiting to be seen, but avoiding the long hauls.

Like an abandoned treehouse, in the forest of the deep.

Looking for that cosy shelter, for a goodnight sleep.

(10 November 2021)

17. Love

Deep, Wide or Scarred
I will always love you
For this is the only truth un barred
For this is the only reality I can derive from you!
Love makes everything achievable,
From the Hardest of objects become pliable,
To the steepest of the climbs doable,
As is the mind, so is my heart, mendable.
Perhaps love is inside everyone,
They do not know it yet,
So find it!, I urge you, lets all of us be one!
As they say! One for all & all for one, everyone :)
Come, lets join HANDS ONLY!
Because our feets are already connected by MOTHER EARTH.
Because our minds are already joined by the force of nothingness (or is it
LOVE :)

(1:57 PM, 15 April 2022)

18. Life Part-1

Life has no meaning as such,
For meaning is something that is ascribed.
Neither to be cherished nor glorified.
Only to wander over one's creative touch.

19. Life

Life may be unkind, deviant or destructive.
Feynman would say, "Nature will reveal itself in whatever form it really
is" Some are reductionists, some are not.
The question is what we do and believe.
Ofcourse Sam Harris will have many things to say about belief.
As he has a PhD on "Belief" I believe.
One can only fathom what lies behind every act or belief.
But what life really is, is not in anyone's gauge.
Perhaps our best rhetoric can only entertain the mind.
But not our hearts.
Even if it does, it does without a master or advisor.
This human form of collection of energy maybe what we are.
But it is our duty to express and perform inquiries, inquisitions and
imaginations.
Maybe life is a way of asking question about life itself.
Personal or impersonal, Perfectly or imperfectly,
We fly in the space of our minds and nature.
Asking without the need for an answer, I think.
But for our scientific hearts, we tend to endorse the physical theories.
As for our artistic soul, we paint the emptiness.
Although our rhetoric minds, we engage in old stories & philosophy.
Perhaps these cocktail of knowledge is nature itself.
And the recognition of these chaos and order is life.
Unknowingly, we continue to exist.

Unaware, we exist to live.
Undoubtedly, we are, allowed.
Allowed,
To ask,
To answer,
To love,
To fight,
To vanish,
To cure,
To finally exist, among all these round planets & accepting for what is,
what was and what perhaps will be.
And, To Just Be

(May 7th, 2022)

20. Lying

Perhaps life is full of lies & truth, the same amount,

Well one cannot immediately figure out,

It must be fun for those who are able

Perhaps they lie on neutral grounds

Waiting for tools to gather.

It is peaceful to lay among valid grounds made of truths

Forever in service of mankind

We will once again unite,

Like that of the movie "Independence day 1996"

We have & We are in some form or shape

With much accretion we ride together

In the tide of time & along with the brilliance of nature

Perhaps it is not in our control to snatch it

Or persuade us from our goals as a species

Us humans lying is also a general human property

(1 : 44 PM, 5th of February 2022)

21. Break

What do you mean by a break?
Is it the mundane specificity?
Or those of unconscious breakage?
I am not sure.
However, I do not know the best & the brightest
Be it stars, universes or multiverses or humans or plants
Let us be friends
& grow together for out of the world
We will & must survive & breakthrough
Not in destruction but in communication

(11: 04 PM, 5th February 2022)

22. Morning laziness

I should have borrowed "mundanity" from James Joyce.
But not all must/should begin where it was,
It can also be programmed or begin from chaos like the Greeks did.
Why waste time arguing with what was,
We can & we must know!
Requoting Hilbert, does not help in consoling the soul
Rather in the midst of unknown burrows,
Human lie without an inkling's care for lost souls
Perhaps, Cantankerous was a word just assigned a horrible meaning to it
Not intended to be a Sonnet, here
Therefore, I end with this self reflection of the title above
Without any thought of solutions or breakthroughs to keep us away from
the morning laziness.

(5 : 27 AM, 30th February 2022)

23. Evidence & Faith

When the empirics allow a change of heart, faith begins its journey
Papers, letters, and words shaping futures,
While forgotten intuitions and missing hands, prove nothing daily
Yet unwritten history passes, leaving only humor.
They say, faith, a rootless tree
But belief rages even among the baseless,
A scented heart, a sharp mind, oh how they disagree
Although both do fill the tapestry of the motionless.
What bridge may this be,
In this contradictory weave
We dance, looking for the next, thinking what it must be,
Accepting this paradox, in the light we thrive.
Making sure this drama reveals itself,
Looking for closure, before we all sleep ourselves.

(10 February, 2022)

Epilogue

Now that you've read the whole book, think about anything and pen it down in a paper or I prefer penzu app. And see what magic your brain has hidden from you. J.K. Rowling said "Imagination is the magic that is endowed upon us humans and we do not need real magic". So imagine, write the shittiest version you can and send it to me I'll read yours too :)